KRISHNA MOHAN AVANCHA

Quora: Lead Generation

This book was professionally typeset on Reedsy.
Find out more at reedsy.com

Contents

1 Introduction to Quora and its potential
  for lead generation   1

2 Understanding the different types of
  leads and their...   3

3 Identifying your target audience on Quora   6

4 Crafting an effective Quora profile for
  lead generation   10

5 Building credibility and authority on Quora   14

6 How to identify and join relevant Quora groups   18

7 Strategies for answering questions to
  generate leads   22

8 Strategies for creating comprehensive
  FAQ page   26

9 Tips for writing effective Quora answers   30

10 Using Quora's search function to find
  potential leads   33

11 The role of keywords in Quora lead generation   37

12 How to use Quora's ad platform for lead generation   41

13 Steps for running ads on Quora   45

14 The benefits of Quora's partner program
  for lead generation   48

15 The role of Quora in your overall lead
  generation strategy   52

16 How to measure the success of your
    Quora lead generation...   55
17 Common mistakes to avoid when using
    Quora for lead...   61
18 How to stay up-to-date with Quora's
    algorithm changes   65
19 The importance of engaging with Quora
    users to generate...   68
20 How to identify and target high-value
    leads on Quora   71
21 Tips for creating compelling Quora con-
    tent that generates...   74
22 The role of Quora in building brand
    awareness and trust   78
23 Strategies for leveraging Quora to drive
    website traffic and...   81
24 How to use Quora to generate leads for
    different industries   84
25 The benefits of collaborating with other
    Quora users for...   87
26 How to use Quora's analytics to track
    your lead generation...   90
27 The role of Quora in B2B lead generation   93
28 The role of Quora in B2C lead generation   95
29 Using Quora to generate leads for B2C businesses 98
30 The importance of personalization in
    Quora lead generation   101
31 How to nurture leads generated on Quora   104
32 The role of Quora in building customer relationships 107
33 Case studies of successful Quora lead
    generation campaigns   109

1

Introduction to Quora and its potential for lead generation

Quora is a social media platform that allows users to ask and answer questions on a wide range of topics. It has become a valuable resource for individuals seeking information and advice on various subjects. However, Quora is more than just a platform for information exchange; it is also a potential goldmine for lead generation.

As a digital marketer, it is essential to understand the potential of Quora as a lead generation tool. With over 300 million active users, Quora provides a vast audience for businesses to tap into. Moreover, Quora has a highly engaged community, with users spending an average of 10-15 minutes on the platform daily.

To leverage Quora's potential for lead generation, businesses need to create a Quora profile and start answering questions related to their industry. By providing helpful and informative answers, businesses can establish themselves as thought leaders in their respective industries, thereby building trust with potential customers.

Businesses can also use Quora's search feature to find questions related to their products or services. By answering these questions and providing valuable information, businesses can attract potential customers to their website or landing page.

Another effective strategy is to create a Quora Space. A Space is a community where users can share knowledge and information about a specific topic. By creating a Space related to their industry, businesses can build a community of like-minded individuals and establish themselves as experts in their field.

Moreover, businesses can use Quora's advertising platform to target potential customers based on their interests and behavior. Quora's advertising platform offers a range of targeting options, including keyword targeting, topic targeting, and behavioral targeting.

In conclusion, Quora offers significant potential for lead generation. By creating a profile, answering questions, creating a Space, and leveraging Quora's advertising platform, businesses can tap into Quora's vast audience and generate high-quality leads. However, it is essential to provide valuable and informative answers and avoid spamming or self-promotion, as this can harm a business's reputation on the platform.

2

Understanding the different types of leads and their importance

As a digital marketer, understanding the different types of leads is crucial for successful lead generation and conversion. Leads are individuals or organizations who have expressed interest in your product or service and can potentially become paying customers. There are several types of leads, each with its own unique characteristics and level of readiness to make a purchase.

1. Marketing Qualified Leads (MQLs)

Marketing Qualified Leads (MQLs) are individuals or organizations who have shown interest in your product or service through marketing efforts, such as filling out a contact form, subscribing to a newsletter, or downloading gated content. MQLs are not necessarily ready to make a purchase, but they have demonstrated some level of engagement with your brand and are worth nurturing further through targeted marketing campaigns.

3

1. Sales Qualified Leads (SQLs)

Sales Qualified Leads (SQLs) are individuals or organizations who have shown a higher level of interest and engagement with your brand and are considered more likely to make a purchase. SQLs typically have interacted with your sales team, either through a consultation call or a demo, and have expressed a specific interest in your product or service.

1. Product Qualified Leads (PQLs)

Product Qualified Leads (PQLs) are individuals or organizations who have already used or interacted with your product or service in some way and have demonstrated a higher level of interest and intention to make a purchase. PQLs may have signed up for a free trial, used a freemium version of your product, or participated in a product demo.

1. Service Qualified Leads (SQLs)

Service Qualified Leads (SQLs) are individuals or organizations who have expressed interest in your services and have initiated contact with your customer support team. SQLs are typically further along in the decision-making process and are more likely to make a purchase.

Each type of lead requires a different approach and level of nurturing. MQLs require targeted marketing campaigns, such as email marketing and retargeting ads, to move them down the funnel. SQLs require personalized sales outreach, such as follow-up calls and personalized demos, to help them make a purchasing decision. PQLs require a more hands-on approach, such as personalized onboarding and product demos, to help them understand the value of your product and make a purchasing decision. SQLs require personalized support and service to ensure they have a positive experience with your brand and become loyal customers.

In conclusion, understanding the different types of leads and their characteristics is crucial for successful lead generation and conversion. By identifying and nurturing the right type of lead, digital marketers can increase their chances of converting leads into paying customers and driving business growth.

3

Identifying your target audience on Quora

Quora is a powerful platform for digital marketers looking to reach new audiences, generate leads, and increase brand awareness. With over 300 million monthly active users, Quora provides a unique opportunity to engage with potential customers, answer their questions, and establish your brand as a thought leader in your industry. However, to maximize the effectiveness of your Quora marketing strategy, it's crucial to identify your target audience on the platform. In this article, we'll explore the key steps you can take to identify and engage with your target audience on Quora.

Step 1: Conduct Market Research

Before you can identify your target audience on Quora, you need to have a deep understanding of your ideal customer. Start by conducting market research to identify the demographics, interests, and pain points of your target audience. This research can include analyzing your existing customer data, surveying your audience, and studying your competitors' customer profiles.

Once you have a clear understanding of your target audience, use this information to create a buyer persona. This persona should represent your ideal customer and include information such as their age, gender, income, education level, job title, interests, and pain points. Having a clear understanding of your buyer persona will help you identify and target your audience on Quora more effectively.

Step 2: Find Relevant Topics

The next step in identifying your target audience on Quora is to find relevant topics. Quora has a wide range of topics covering everything from technology to cooking to fashion. To find topics that are relevant to your target audience, start by searching for keywords related to your industry or niche.

For example, if you sell skincare products, you could search for topics related to skincare, beauty, and self-care. Once you've found relevant topics, browse through the questions and answers to identify the most popular and relevant content. This will give you a better understanding of the types of questions your target audience is asking and the information they're seeking.

Step 3: Analyze User Behavior

Quora provides a wealth of data on user behavior, including the questions they ask, the answers they read, and the topics they follow. Analyzing this data can help you identify patterns and trends in user behavior, which can help you target your audience more effectively.

Start by analyzing the questions that your target audience is asking. Look for common themes, pain points, and topics that are of particular interest to your audience. This will help you create content that addresses their specific needs and interests.

7

You can also analyze the answers that your target audience is reading. Look for the most upvoted and shared answers, as these tend to be the most informative and helpful. This will give you an idea of the type of content that resonates with your target audience.

Finally, analyze the topics that your target audience is following. This will give you an idea of their broader interests and can help you identify other topics and niches that may be relevant to your brand.

Step 4: Engage with Your Target Audience

Once you've identified your target audience on Quora, it's time to engage with them. Start by answering questions related to your industry or niche. Make sure your answers are informative, helpful, and provide value to the user.

You can also create content on Quora, such as blog posts, guides, and tutorials. This content should be relevant to your target audience and address their specific needs and interests.

Another effective way to engage with your target audience is to participate in Quora's community features, such as comments and upvotes. This will help you establish yourself as a thought leader in your industry and build relationships with potential customers.

Step 5: Measure Your Results

Measuring the results of your Quora marketing strategy is crucial to understanding its effectiveness and identifying areas for improvement. Here are some key steps to help you measure your results on Quora:

1. Set goals: Before you start measuring your results, you need to have clear goals in mind. These goals could

include increasing website traffic, generating leads, or increasing brand awareness. Having clear goals will help you focus your efforts and measure the success of your Quora marketing strategy more effectively.

2. Use Quora Analytics: Quora provides a range of analytics tools that can help you measure the effectiveness of your content and engagement on the platform. Quora Analytics allows you to track metrics such as views, upvotes, shares, and followers, giving you a better understanding of how your content is performing and how users are engaging with your brand.

3. Use Google Analytics: In addition to Quora Analytics, you should also use Google Analytics to measure the impact of your Quora marketing strategy on your website. By tracking metrics such as referral traffic and conversions, you can see how Quora is driving users to your website and whether these users are converting into customers.

4. Analyze your results: Once you have collected data on your Quora marketing strategy, it's important to analyze it to identify patterns, trends, and areas for improvement. Look for areas where you are seeing success and areas where you may need to adjust your strategy.

5. Adjust your strategy: Based on your analysis, adjust your Quora marketing strategy to better meet the needs and interests of your target audience. This may involve creating more targeted content, engaging with users more effectively, or targeting different topics or niches.

By measuring your results on Quora, you can optimize your marketing strategy, increase your ROI, and drive better results for your business.

4

Crafting an effective Quora profile for lead generation

Q uora is a powerful social media platform that has revolutionized the way people seek and share information. As a digital marketer, it presents a unique opportunity to connect with potential customers by answering questions in your area of expertise. However, to maximize the platform's potential, you need to have a well-crafted Quora profile. This guide will show you how to create an effective Quora profile for lead generation.

- Start with a clear and concise bio

Your Quora bio is the first thing people will see when they come across your profile. It should be clear, concise, and engaging. Start with a brief introduction about yourself and what you do. Then, mention your area of expertise and what topics you are knowledgeable about. Use keywords related to your industry to make it easier for people to find you.

Your bio should also convey your personality and style. This will help people relate to you and trust you. For example, if you're a creative marketer, you could write your bio in a witty and humorous style.

- Add a professional profile picture

Your profile picture is an important part of your Quora profile. It should be a professional headshot that showcases your personality and expertise. Avoid using casual photos or selfies. A professional profile picture will help build trust and credibility with potential leads.

- Showcase your expertise in your credentials

Your credentials section is where you can highlight your achievements, awards, and credentials. This section can include your education, certifications, work experience, and any other relevant information. This will help establish your expertise in your industry and increase your credibility with potential leads.

- Create a keyword-rich profile description

Your profile description is an important element in your Quora profile. It is an opportunity to showcase your expertise and attract potential leads. Use keywords related to your industry to optimize your profile for search engines. This will help your profile show up when people search for topics related to your expertise.

Your profile description should also be engaging and informative. It should showcase your personality and style while

11

providing value to your potential leads. Use a conversational tone and avoid using jargon or technical terms that may be unfamiliar to your audience.

• Add links to your website and social media profiles

Your Quora profile is a great place to drive traffic to your website and social media profiles. Include links to your website and social media profiles in your Quora profile. This will help potential leads learn more about you and your business.

• Answer questions in your area of expertise

Once you have created a well-crafted Quora profile, it's time to start answering questions in your area of expertise. Look for questions related to your industry and provide thoughtful and informative answers. Use your expertise and experience to provide valuable insights to your audience.

When answering questions, make sure to include a brief bio at the end of your answer. This will help potential leads learn more about you and your business. You can also include a call-to-action (CTA) that encourages people to visit your website or contact you for more information.

• Engage with your audience

Engaging with your audience is an important part of lead generation on Quora. Respond to comments on your answers and engage in conversations with your audience. This will help build trust and establish you as an authority in your industry.

Engaging with your audience can also help you identify

potential leads. Look for people who are asking questions related to your area of expertise and engage with them. This can help establish a relationship with potential leads and increase the chances of converting them into customers.

- Monitor your analytics

Monitoring your analytics is an important part of lead generation on Quora. Keep track of how your answers are performing and which topics are generating the most engagement. This will help you identify trends and optimize your strategy for maximum effectiveness.

5

Building credibility and authority on Quora

A s a digital marketer, I can attest to the power of Quora for building credibility and authority within a given industry. Quora is a popular question-and-answer platform where people can ask and answer questions on any topic. The platform has over 300 million monthly active users, making it a valuable tool for businesses looking to establish themselves as thought leaders in their respective fields.

Here are some strategies for building credibility and authority on Quora:

- Choose your topics wisely

Quora has a wide range of topics, from science and technology to politics and sports. When choosing which topics to answer questions in, it's important to select ones that are relevant to your industry and expertise. This will help you to establish yourself as an authority on the subject and attract more views and followers.

- Provide valuable and insightful answers

The key to building credibility and authority on Quora is to provide valuable and insightful answers to questions. Avoid generic or vague answers and instead provide specific and detailed information. Use real-life examples, case studies, and statistics to support your answers. This will help to establish you as a credible source of information and attract more upvotes and followers.

- Use visuals and multimedia

Visuals and multimedia can make your answers more engaging and memorable. Use images, videos, infographics, and other types of multimedia to help illustrate your points and make your answers more appealing to readers. This will help to increase the chances of your answers being shared and followed.

- Be consistent

Consistency is key when it comes to building credibility and authority on Quora. Answer questions regularly and consistently, and aim to provide high-quality answers each time. This will help to establish you as a reliable and trustworthy source of information, and attract more followers to your profile.

- Engage with the Quora community

Engaging with the Quora community is a great way to build credibility and authority on the platform. Respond to comments and questions, upvote other users' answers, and follow other users who share similar interests or expertise. This will help to establish you as an active member of the community and attract more followers to your profile.

- Share your Quora content on social media

Sharing your Quora content on social media can help to increase its reach and attract more followers to your profile. Share your answers on platforms like Twitter, LinkedIn, and Facebook, and encourage your followers to engage with your content. This will help to establish you as an authority on your topic outside of Quora and attract more followers to your profile.

- Use Quora Ads to promote your content

Quora Ads is a powerful advertising platform that can help to promote your content and increase your visibility on the platform. Use Quora Ads to promote your answers to relevant questions or target users based on their interests and behavior. This will help to increase your visibility on the platform and attract more followers to your profile.

- Participate in Quora Spaces

Quora Spaces is a feature that allows users to create and join communities around specific topics. Participating in Quora Spaces can help to increase your visibility and credibility within your industry, and attract more followers to your profile. Join relevant Spaces, engage with other members, and share your expertise to establish yourself as a thought leader in your field.

In conclusion, building credibility and authority on Quora requires a combination of strategies and tactics. By choosing your topics wisely, providing valuable and insightful answers, using visuals and multimedia, being consistent, engaging with the Quora community, sharing your content on social media, using Quora Ads, and participating in Quora Spaces, you can establish yourself as a thought leader in your industry and attract more followers to your profile. With the right approach and effort, Quora can be a powerful tool for building credibility and authority in the digital marketing world.

6

How to identify and join relevant Quora groups

As a digital marketer, one of the best ways to establish yourself as an expert in your industry and build your brand is by participating in relevant online communities. One such community that has gained immense popularity in recent years is Quora. It is a question-and-answer platform that enables users to ask and answer questions on a wide range of topics.

Quora has over 300 million monthly active users, making it a great platform for marketers to reach a large audience. But with so many users and topics, it can be challenging to find and join the most relevant groups to your niche. Here are some tips on how to identify and join relevant Quora groups:

- Identify your target audience

The first step in identifying relevant Quora groups is to understand your target audience. Who are the people you want to reach, and what are their interests and pain points? Once you have a clear understanding of your target audience, you can start searching for Quora groups that match their interests.

For example, if your target audience is small business owners, you can search for Quora groups related to entrepreneurship, marketing, and business management.

• Search for groups using keywords

Quora's search function is a powerful tool that can help you find relevant groups. Start by using keywords related to your niche to search for relevant topics and questions. Once you find a question or topic that matches your niche, you can check the groups associated with it.

For example, if you're in the fitness industry, you can search for keywords such as "workout routines," "healthy eating," or "fitness tips" to find relevant topics and questions. From there, you can explore the groups related to those topics.

• Explore related topics

Another way to find relevant Quora groups is to explore related topics. Quora's algorithm suggests related topics based on the questions and topics you have engaged with in the past. You can use this feature to find new topics and groups that match your niche.

For example, if you are interested in social media marketing, you can explore related topics such as "content marketing," "digital marketing," and "social media advertising." This will help you discover new groups that you might not have found otherwise.

- Look for active groups

When joining Quora groups, it's essential to look for active groups. Active groups are those that have a lot of engagement, including questions, answers, and discussions. These groups are more likely to have a dedicated audience and provide more opportunities for networking and collaboration.

You can identify active groups by looking at the number of members, the frequency of posts and discussions, and the quality of the content. You can also look at the group's stats, which provide information on how many questions have been asked and how many answers have been given.

- Join relevant groups

Once you have identified relevant Quora groups, it's time to join them. Before joining a group, make sure you read the group's description and rules to ensure that it is relevant to your niche and that you understand the group's guidelines.

When joining a group, introduce yourself and let other members know your expertise and interests. You can also engage with existing posts and questions to build relationships and establish yourself as an expert in your field.

- Participate actively

To get the most out of Quora groups, it's essential to participate actively. This means asking questions, answering questions, and engaging with other members' posts. By participating actively, you can establish yourself as an expert in your field and build relationships with other members.

When participating in groups, it's crucial to provide value to other members. This means sharing your knowledge and expertise and providing helpful answers and insights. By providing value, you can build trust and credibility with other members, which can lead to new opportunities and collaborations.

7

Strategies for answering questions to generate leads

I n the world of digital marketing, lead generation is an
essential part of any successful marketing strategy. A lead
is a potential customer who has shown interest in your
product or service, and it is the job of the marketer to turn that
interest into a sale. One effective way to generate leads is by
answering questions related to your product or service. Here
are some strategies for answering questions to generate leads:

- Identify the most commonly asked questions

The first step in answering questions to generate leads is to
identify the most commonly asked questions related to your
product or service. This can be done by analyzing customer
feedback, reviewing customer support requests, or conducting
a survey. Once you have identified the most common questions,
you can create content that directly answers those questions.

- Create a comprehensive FAQ page

Creating a comprehensive FAQ (Frequently Asked Questions) page is an effective way to provide answers to potential customers. Make sure your FAQ page includes all the essential information about your product or service, such as pricing, features, and benefits. Use clear and concise language and avoid using technical jargon that may confuse the reader.

- Use social media to answer questions

Social media is an excellent platform for answering questions and generating leads. Monitor your social media accounts for questions related to your product or service and respond promptly. Make sure your responses are informative and helpful. If you can't answer the question immediately, let the customer know you are looking into it and will get back to them as soon as possible.

- Use live chat to answer questions

Live chat is another effective way to answer questions and generate leads. Many customers prefer live chat because it provides an immediate response. Make sure your live chat feature is easy to access and available during business hours. Train your live chat agents to provide helpful and informative responses to potential customers.

- Create educational content

Creating educational content, such as blog posts, videos, and webinars, is an effective way to answer questions and generate leads. Your content should be informative, engaging, and relevant to your target audience. Use clear and concise language and provide examples to illustrate your points. Include a call-to-action at the end of your content to encourage potential customers to take the next step.

• Use targeted advertising

Targeted advertising is an effective way to reach potential customers who are asking questions related to your product or service. Use keywords related to your product or service to target your ads to people who are actively searching for answers. Make sure your ad copy is informative and provides a clear call-to-action.

• Engage with industry influencers

Engaging with industry influencers is an effective way to answer questions and generate leads. Identify influencers in your industry and engage with them on social media. Share their content, comment on their posts, and ask questions. This will help you build a relationship with the influencer, which can lead to them promoting your product or service to their followers.

• Use customer reviews to answer questions

Customer reviews are an excellent source of information for potential customers. Use customer reviews to answer questions related to your product or service. If a customer asks a question in a review, respond promptly and provide a helpful answer. Use customer reviews as a way to showcase the benefits of your product or service.

- Provide excellent customer service

Providing excellent customer service is essential for generating leads. Make sure your customer service team is trained to answer questions related to your product or service. Respond promptly to customer inquiries and provide helpful and informative responses. If a customer has a negative experience, take steps to resolve the issue quickly and effectively.

In conclusion, answering questions related to your product or service is an effective way to generate leads. Use the strategies outlined above to provide helpful and informative answers to potential customers.

8

Strategies for creating comprehensive FAQ page

A Frequently Asked Questions (FAQ) page is an essential part of any website, particularly for businesses. This page can help reduce the number of inquiries or customer service calls received by a company, which ultimately saves time and resources. However, creating a comprehensive FAQ page takes more than just listing questions and answers. To make the most of your FAQ page, you need to strategize.

In this article, I will provide you with strategies for creating a comprehensive FAQ page that will help your visitors and customers find what they are looking for quickly and easily.

- Identify Your Target Audience and Their Needs

The first step in creating a comprehensive FAQ page is to identify your target audience and their needs. You need to understand the types of questions your customers ask and what they are looking for in terms of information. This information will help you create a relevant and useful FAQ page that meets their needs.

To identify your target audience's needs, you can start by reviewing your customer service logs and social media interactions. Take note of the most common questions or issues that your customers ask. This information will help you determine the content to include in your FAQ page.

- Organize Your FAQ Page

The next step is to organize your FAQ page. A well-organized FAQ page will make it easier for visitors to find the information they are looking for quickly. You can organize your FAQ page in different ways, including by topic, category, or product.

If you have a large FAQ page, you may want to consider using a search function to make it easier for visitors to find what they are looking for. You can also use subheadings, bullet points, and tables to make your FAQ page more organized and user-friendly.

- Use Clear and Simple Language

One of the most important strategies for creating a comprehensive FAQ page is to use clear and simple language. Your FAQ page should be easy to read and understand. Avoid using technical jargon or complex language that may confuse your visitors.

Use simple language to explain complex concepts or processes. Use short sentences and avoid using long paragraphs. You can also use images and videos to make your FAQ page more engaging and easier to understand.

- Anticipate and Answer Common Questions

Your FAQ page should include answers to the most common questions or issues that your customers have. This will help reduce the number of inquiries or customer service calls you receive. Anticipate the questions that your customers may have and provide clear and concise answers.

It's also important to update your FAQ page regularly. As your business evolves, new products or services may be introduced, and customer needs may change. Update your FAQ page to reflect these changes and address new questions that may arise.

- Use Analytics to Optimize Your FAQ Page

Finally, you can use analytics to optimize your FAQ page. Analytics can help you track how visitors interact with your FAQ page, including which questions are most frequently asked, which pages are most viewed, and how long visitors spend on your FAQ page.

Use this information to identify areas where your FAQ page can be improved. You can also use A/B testing to test different versions of your FAQ page and see which version performs better.

In conclusion, a comprehensive FAQ page is an essential part of any website, particularly for businesses. To create a useful and effective FAQ page, you need to identify your target audience's needs, organize your FAQ page, use clear and simple language, anticipate and answer common questions, and use analytics to optimize your FAQ page. With these strategies in mind, you can create a comprehensive FAQ page that will help your visitors and customers find what they are looking for quickly and easily.

9

Tips for writing effective Quora answers

Quora is a popular question-and-answer platform that has become a valuable resource for digital marketers. Not only does Quora provide a platform for marketers to showcase their expertise, but it also serves as a means to connect with potential customers and build brand awareness.

Writing effective Quora answers requires a strategic approach. Here are some tips for digital marketers to keep in mind when crafting their responses:

- Choose the right questions to answer

The first step in writing effective Quora answers is to choose the right questions to answer. Look for questions that are relevant to your industry, and that you have expertise in. You should also look for questions that have a high number of views, as these questions are more likely to be seen by a larger audience.

- Provide valuable information

When writing Quora answers, it's important to provide valuable information that answers the question in a clear and concise manner. Be sure to provide detailed information, but avoid being overly technical or using jargon that might confuse the reader. Also, avoid providing generic responses that don't add any value to the conversation.

- Use storytelling

Storytelling is a powerful tool that can be used to engage readers and make your answers more memorable. When answering questions on Quora, try to incorporate stories or anecdotes that illustrate your point. This will make your answers more interesting and engaging, and will help to build trust with your audience.

- Be authentic

Authenticity is key when it comes to writing effective Quora answers. Don't be afraid to share your personal experiences or opinions, as this can help to build a connection with your audience. However, be sure to back up your opinions with data or examples, as this will add credibility to your answers.

- Use visuals

Visuals can help to break up text and make your answers more engaging. Consider including images, infographics, or videos in your answers to help illustrate your points. Just be sure that the visuals you choose are relevant to the question being asked, and don't distract from the main message of your answer.

• Focus on formatting

Formatting is an important consideration when writing Quora answers. Use bullet points or numbered lists to break up text and make your answers easier to read. Also, consider using bold or italicized text to highlight key points or important information.

• Include a call to action

Finally, be sure to include a call to action in your Quora answers. This could be as simple as asking the reader to visit your website for more information, or inviting them to connect with you on social media. Including a call to action can help to drive traffic to your website or social media profiles, and can help to convert Quora users into customers.

In summary, writing effective Quora answers requires a strategic approach. Choose the right questions to answer, provide valuable information, use storytelling, be authentic, use visuals, focus on formatting, and include a call to action. By following these tips, digital marketers can use Quora to build brand awareness, connect with potential customers, and showcase their expertise.

10

Using Quora's search function to find potential leads

Quora is a powerful social media platform that is often overlooked by digital marketers. Quora allows users to ask and answer questions on a wide variety of topics, making it a great resource for finding potential leads. In this article, we will discuss how to use Quora's search function to find potential leads and how to convert those leads into customers.

- Understanding Quora's Search Function

The first step in using Quora to find potential leads is to understand how Quora's search function works. Quora's search function is similar to other search engines like Google. You can type in keywords related to your business or industry, and Quora will return a list of questions that are related to those keywords. The search function is located at the top of the Quora homepage, and you can enter any keyword or phrase related to your industry to find relevant questions.

- Finding Relevant Questions

Once you have entered your keyword or phrase into the search bar, Quora will return a list of questions related to that keyword. It is important to find questions that are relevant to your business or industry. You can do this by reading the question and the answers that have been provided. Look for questions that have a high number of views or upvotes, as this indicates that the question is popular and has a large audience.

- Providing Value

The key to using Quora to find potential leads is to provide value to the Quora community. This means answering questions with high-quality answers that are informative and helpful. When you provide value to the Quora community, people will start to view you as an expert in your field. This can lead to increased visibility and credibility for your business, which can ultimately lead to more leads and customers.

- Engaging with the Community

Another important aspect of using Quora to find potential leads is to engage with the community. This means following other users, commenting on their answers, and upvoting answers that you find helpful. Engaging with the Quora community is a great way to build relationships and establish yourself as an expert in your field.

- Building Your Profile

Your Quora profile is an important tool for building your brand and establishing yourself as an expert in your field. Make sure that your profile is complete and includes a professional profile picture and bio. You can also link to your website or social media profiles to drive traffic and increase visibility for your business.

- Converting Leads into Customers

Once you have found potential leads on Quora, the next step is to convert those leads into customers. One way to do this is to include a call-to-action (CTA) in your answers. For example, you could offer a free consultation or a discount code for your product or service. You could also include a link to your website or social media profiles where potential leads can learn more about your business.

- Tracking Your Results

Finally, it is important to track your results and measure the effectiveness of your Quora marketing strategy. You can track the number of views, upvotes, and comments on your answers to see how your content is performing. You can also track the number of leads and customers that you are generating from Quora to measure the ROI of your efforts.

Conclusion

Using Quora's search function to find potential leads is a powerful strategy for digital marketers. By providing value to the Quora community, engaging with other users, and building your profile, you can establish yourself as an expert in your field and generate more leads and customers for your business.

With the right approach and a little bit of effort, Quora can be a valuable tool for any digital marketing strategy.

11

The role of keywords in Quora lead generation

As a digital marketer with extensive experience, I understand the importance of keywords in any marketing strategy. When it comes to lead generation on Quora, keywords play a crucial role in attracting potential customers and driving conversions. In this article, I will discuss the role of keywords in Quora lead generation and provide some tips for optimizing your keyword strategy.

What are Keywords?

Keywords are words or phrases that people use to search for information on the internet. In the context of Quora, keywords are the terms that people use to find and engage with content related to their interests. By using the right keywords in your Quora content, you can attract the right audience and increase your chances of generating leads.

Why are Keywords important for Quora lead generation?

Quora is a platform where people come to find answers to their questions. As a digital marketer, your goal is to provide the answers that your potential customers are looking for. This is where keywords come in. By including the right keywords in your Quora content, you can make sure that your answers appear in the search results when people search for those keywords.

In addition to helping you reach the right audience, keywords also help you establish credibility and authority on Quora. When you provide helpful and informative answers that are relevant to your target audience, you increase your chances of earning their trust and building a relationship with them. This, in turn, can lead to more conversions and higher ROI.

Tips for Optimizing Your Keyword Strategy for Quora Lead Generation

1. Do Your Research

The first step in optimizing your keyword strategy for Quora lead generation is to do your research. Start by identifying the keywords that are most relevant to your business and your target audience. Use keyword research tools like Google AdWords Keyword Planner or SEMrush to find keywords that have a high search volume and low competition.

1. Focus on Long-Tail Keywords

When it comes to Quora lead generation, long-tail keywords are your best friend. These are keywords that are more specific and less competitive than generic keywords. For example, instead of targeting the keyword "digital marketing," you might target the long-tail keyword "how to improve your digital marketing strategy." By focusing on long-tail keywords, you can attract a more targeted audience and increase your chances of generating high-quality leads.

1. Use Keywords in Your Quora Profile

Your Quora profile is an important part of your overall marketing strategy. Make sure that you include relevant keywords in your profile description and in the topics that you follow. This will help you attract the right audience and establish yourself as an authority in your field.

1. Include Keywords in Your Answers

When answering questions on Quora, make sure that you include relevant keywords in your answers. This will help your answers appear in the search results when people search for those keywords. However, make sure that you don't stuff your answers with keywords. Your answers should be helpful and informative first and foremost.

1. Use Keyword Variations

Don't just focus on one keyword. Use variations of your main keywords throughout your Quora content. This will help you attract a wider audience and increase your chances of generating more leads.

1. Monitor Your Results

Finally, make sure that you monitor your results and adjust your keyword strategy accordingly. Use analytics tools like Google Analytics or Quora's built-in analytics to track your traffic and conversion rates. If you're not seeing the results that you want, adjust your keywords and try again.

Conclusion

Keywords are an essential part of any digital marketing strategy, and they play a crucial role in Quora lead generation. By using the right keywords in your Quora content, you can attract the right audience, establish credibility and authority, and increase your chances of generating high-quality leads.

12

How to use Quora's ad platform for lead generation

Q uora is a popular question-and-answer website that has grown to become one of the top platforms for marketers to generate leads. With its large user base, engaged audience, and sophisticated targeting capabilities, Quora is a powerful tool for businesses looking to drive high-quality leads and increase their online visibility. In this article, we'll take a look at how you can use Quora's ad platform for lead generation.

- Set up your Quora ad account

The first step in using Quora's ad platform for lead generation is to create your account. You can sign up for a Quora Ads account by visiting the Quora Ads website and clicking the "Get Started" button. You'll then be prompted to enter your company information and payment details.

- Choose your ad type

Quora offers two main types of ads: text ads and promoted answers. Text ads are similar to Google AdWords ads and appear at the top of the page, while promoted answers are answers to questions that are promoted to the top of the page. For lead generation purposes, we recommend using text ads as they allow for more targeted messaging and better tracking of conversions.

- Define your target audience

One of the key advantages of Quora's ad platform is its sophisticated targeting capabilities. You can target your ads based on a variety of factors, including keywords, topics, location, device, and more. To generate high-quality leads, it's important to define your target audience carefully. Think about who your ideal customer is and what questions they might be asking on Quora. Use this information to create a list of keywords and topics that you want to target with your ads.

- Write your ad copy

The next step is to create your ad copy. Your ad copy should be concise, engaging, and relevant to the audience you are targeting. Highlight the benefits of your product or service and include a strong call-to-action that encourages users to click on your ad. Quora's ad platform allows for up to 105 characters for the headline and up to 175 characters for the ad description, so make every word count.

- Set your budget and bidding strategy

42

Quora's ad platform works on a cost-per-click (CPC) basis, which means you only pay when someone clicks on your ad. You can set a daily budget for your campaign and a bid for each click. Quora offers two bidding strategies: automatic and manual. Automatic bidding lets Quora set the bid for you based on your budget and goals, while manual bidding lets you set your own bid. To optimize your lead generation efforts, we recommend starting with manual bidding and adjusting your bid based on the performance of your ads.

- Monitor and optimize your campaign

Once your ads are up and running, it's important to monitor their performance and make adjustments as needed. Use Quora's analytics tools to track the number of clicks, impressions, and conversions your ads are generating. Identify which ads and targeting strategies are performing best and adjust your campaign accordingly. This may include changing your ad copy, adjusting your targeting, or increasing your bid.

- Retarget your audience

Retargeting is a powerful strategy for generating leads on Quora. By targeting users who have already interacted with your brand, you can increase the chances of converting them into customers. Quora allows you to create a retargeting audience based on users who have visited your website, engaged with your content, or taken a specific action. Use this audience to create targeted ads that speak to their specific needs and interests.

In conclusion, Quora's ad platform is a valuable tool for lead generation. By following these tips and best practices, you can create highly targeted ads that drive high-quality leads and increase your online visibility.

13

Steps for running ads on Quora

Quora is one of the most popular and effective platforms for online marketing. With over 300 million monthly active users, it provides a unique opportunity for businesses to connect with their target audience and promote their products or services. Quora Ads is the platform's native advertising system, which enables marketers to reach out to their audience and engage with them in a meaningful way. In this article, we will discuss the steps for running Quora Ads and how you can leverage this powerful platform for your business.

1. Set up your Quora Ads account: The first step in running Quora Ads is to create an account. To do this, you need to sign up for a Quora Ads account, which is free and easy to do. Once you have created an account, you need to complete your profile by providing your business information, including your name, company name, and contact details. You can also choose your preferred payment method, such as credit card or PayPal.

2. Choose your ad objective: The next step in running Quora

Ads is to choose your ad objective. This will depend on the specific goal you want to achieve, such as driving website traffic, generating leads, or increasing brand awareness. Quora Ads provides a range of ad objectives to choose from, so it is important to select the one that aligns with your marketing goals.

3. Define your target audience: One of the key advantages of Quora Ads is its ability to target specific audiences. To create a successful campaign, you need to define your target audience by selecting relevant topics, interests, and behaviors. You can also target users based on their location, device, and language. Quora Ads provides a range of targeting options to choose from, so it is important to select the ones that align with your audience's interests and behaviors.

4. Set your budget and bid: The next step in running Quora Ads is to set your budget and bid. You need to decide how much you want to spend on your campaign and how much you are willing to pay for each click or impression. Quora Ads uses an auction system, which means that the highest bidder will get the most impressions. It is important to set your bid high enough to get your ad seen by your target audience, but not too high that it eats up your budget.

5. Create your ad: Once you have defined your target audience and set your budget, you need to create your ad. Quora Ads provides a range of ad formats to choose from, such as text, image, and video ads. You need to create an ad that is visually appealing, relevant, and engaging to your target audience. It is important to use high-quality images or videos and compelling ad copy that highlights the benefits of your product or service.

6. Launch your campaign: The final step in running Quora Ads is to launch your campaign. You need to review your ad and make sure it is aligned with your marketing goals and target audience. Once you are satisfied with your ad, you can launch your campaign and start reaching out to your target audience. It is important to monitor your campaign regularly and adjust your budget and bid based on the performance of your ad.

In conclusion, Quora Ads is a powerful platform for digital marketers to promote their products or services and engage with their target audience. By following these steps, you can create a successful Quora Ads campaign that drives website traffic, generates leads, and increases brand awareness. Remember to define your target audience, set your budget and bid, create a visually appealing ad, and launch your campaign. With these steps in mind, you can leverage the power of Quora Ads to grow your business and reach new heights of success.

14

The benefits of Quora's partner program for lead generation

Quora is a popular question-and-answer platform where individuals can ask and answer questions on various topics. The platform has grown in popularity over the years and has become a great resource for individuals seeking information on a wide range of subjects. However, Quora is not just a platform for knowledge sharing, it can also be used as a powerful lead generation tool through its Partner Program.

The Quora Partner Program is a feature that allows businesses to create and publish sponsored content on the Quora platform. By doing so, businesses can reach out to potential customers who are actively seeking information related to their products or services. In this article, we will explore the benefits of the Quora Partner Program for lead generation.

1. Targeted audience One of the biggest advantages of the Quora Partner Program is that it provides businesses with access to a highly targeted audience. Users on Quora are there to ask and answer questions on specific topics. As

a result, businesses can use the platform to reach out to people who are interested in their products or services.

For example, if you are a company that sells software for small businesses, you can create content that targets users who are interested in small business software. This will ensure that your sponsored content is being shown to people who are most likely to be interested in your product, increasing the chances of generating high-quality leads.

1. Cost-effective The Quora Partner Program is a cost-effective way to generate leads for your business. Compared to other forms of advertising, such as Google Ads or Facebook Ads, the cost per click on Quora is relatively low. This means that businesses can get more bang for their buck when it comes to generating leads.

In addition, businesses can set their own budget and only pay when someone clicks on their sponsored content. This ensures that businesses are only paying for leads that have shown genuine interest in their products or services.

1. Increased brand exposure Another benefit of the Quora Partner Program is that it can help increase brand exposure. When businesses create sponsored content on Quora, their brand is displayed prominently in front of potential customers who are actively seeking information related to their products or services.

This increased exposure can help businesses establish themselves as thought leaders in their industry and build trust with potential customers. By consistently creating high-quality content that provides value to users, businesses can position themselves as experts in their field and increase their chances of generating leads.

1. High-quality leads The Quora Partner Program is an excellent way to generate high-quality leads for your business. Users on Quora are actively seeking information on specific topics, which means that businesses can reach out to people who are most likely to be interested in their products or services.

In addition, Quora allows businesses to target their sponsored content to specific demographics, such as location, age, and interests. This ensures that businesses are reaching out to people who are most likely to become paying customers.

1. Measurable results Another benefit of the Quora Partner Program is that it provides businesses with measurable results. Quora offers a variety of analytics tools that businesses can use to track the performance of their sponsored content.

Businesses can track metrics such as clicks, impressions, and conversions, which allows them to optimize their campaigns for maximum effectiveness. By analyzing the data provided by Quora, businesses can identify what is working and what is not, and make changes to their campaigns accordingly.

1. Improved SEO Finally, the Quora Partner Program can help businesses improve their search engine optimization

(SEO). When businesses create high-quality content on Quora, it can help them rank higher in search engine results pages (SERPs).

This is because Quora is a high-authority website, and backlinks from Quora to a business's website can improve its SEO.

15

The role of Quora in your overall lead generation strategy

Q uora is a question-and-answer platform where users can ask questions on any topic and receive answers from the community. As a digital marketer, Quora can be an invaluable tool in your overall lead generation strategy. In this article, we will discuss the role of Quora in lead generation and how you can use it effectively to generate high-quality leads for your business.

- Establishing Yourself as a Thought Leader One of the most significant benefits of using Quora as a digital marketer is that it allows you to establish yourself as a thought leader in your industry. By answering questions related to your field, you can showcase your expertise and provide value to the Quora community. This can help build your credibility and authority, making it more likely that people will trust your brand and become interested in your products or services.

To establish yourself as a thought leader on Quora, you should aim to provide thorough, well-researched answers to questions in your niche. Be sure to use clear, concise language and provide examples and sources to support your points. You can also include links to your website or blog in your answers, which can help drive traffic and leads to your site.

- Building Brand Awareness Quora is a popular platform with over 300 million active monthly users, which means it can be an excellent place to build brand awareness. By answering questions related to your business, you can reach a large audience of potential customers and introduce them to your brand.

To build brand awareness on Quora, you should focus on answering questions that are relevant to your industry and target audience. Be sure to use language and tone that aligns with your brand voice and include your brand name and logo in your profile and answers.

- Targeting Specific Audiences One of the key advantages of using Quora as a digital marketer is that it allows you to target specific audiences. Quora users can ask questions on a wide range of topics, which means you can identify questions related to your niche and provide targeted answers to the people who are most likely to be interested in your products or services.

To target specific audiences on Quora, you should focus on answering questions that are relevant to your target market. You can use Quora's search function to find questions related to your industry or use keywords to identify questions that are likely to be of interest to your target audience.

- Generating High-Quality Leads Ultimately, the goal of any lead generation strategy is to generate high-quality leads that are likely to convert into customers. Quora can be an effective tool for generating leads because it allows you to reach a large audience of potential customers who are actively seeking information related to your industry.

To generate high-quality leads on Quora, you should focus on providing valuable, informative answers to questions in your niche. Be sure to include a call-to-action in your answers, such as inviting people to visit your website or sign up for your newsletter. You can also use Quora's lead generation forms to capture contact information from people who are interested in your products or services.

- Integrating Quora with Your Other Marketing Channels To get the most out of Quora as a lead generation tool, it's important to integrate it with your other marketing channels. You can use Quora to drive traffic to your website or blog, promote your social media profiles, or even run targeted ads to Quora users who are likely to be interested in your products or services.

To integrate Quora with your other marketing channels, you should include links to your website or social media profiles in your Quora profile and answers. You can also use Quora's ad platform to run targeted ads to people who have engaged with your brand on Quora or who are likely to be interested in your products or services.

16

How to measure the success of your Quora lead generation efforts

Q uora is a popular social networking site that allows users to ask and answer questions on a wide range of topics. With over 300 million monthly active users, Quora provides an excellent platform for businesses to generate leads and engage with potential customers. However, as with any marketing effort, it is essential to measure the success of your Quora lead generation efforts to determine their effectiveness and make data-driven decisions to optimize your strategy. In this article, I will discuss how to measure the success of your Quora lead generation efforts and improve your ROI.

- Determine your KPIs

The first step in measuring the success of your Quora lead generation efforts is to determine your key performance indicators (KPIs). KPIs are the metrics that you will use to evaluate the effectiveness of your strategy. Some common KPIs for Quora lead generation include:

- Number of leads generated
- Cost per lead
- Conversion rate
- Engagement rate
- Click-through rate (CTR)
- Return on investment (ROI)

Once you have identified your KPIs, you can track them using tools such as Google Analytics or Quora's native analytics dashboard.

- Set up tracking

To accurately measure your KPIs, you need to set up tracking on your Quora lead generation campaigns. This involves adding tracking URLs to your Quora ads, which will enable you to track clicks and conversions. You can use tools such as Google's Campaign URL Builder to create tracking URLs.

In addition to tracking URLs, you should also set up conversion tracking in Google Analytics or another analytics platform. This will allow you to track the actions that users take on your website after clicking on your Quora ads, such as form submissions or product purchases.

- Monitor your metrics

Once you have set up tracking, you can begin monitoring your metrics. Regular monitoring will enable you to quickly identify any issues with your strategy and make data-driven decisions to optimize your campaigns. You should monitor your metrics at least once a week, if not more frequently.

Some of the metrics you should monitor include:

- Impressions: The number of times your Quora ads were shown to users
- Clicks: The number of times users clicked on your Quora ads
- Conversions: The number of users who completed a desired action, such as filling out a form or making a purchase
- Cost per click (CPC): The amount you pay for each click on your Quora ads
- Cost per conversion (CPA): The amount you pay for each conversion
- Conversion rate: The percentage of users who clicked on your Quora ads and then completed a desired action
- Return on investment (ROI): The revenue generated from your Quora lead generation efforts divided by the cost of those efforts

1. Test and optimize

One of the most important aspects of measuring the success of your Quora lead generation efforts is testing and optimizing your campaigns. Testing involves making small changes to your campaigns and measuring the impact of those changes on your KPIs.

Some elements of your campaigns that you can test include:

- Ad copy: Test different headlines and descriptions to see

57

which ones resonate best with your target audience.
- Targeting: Test different targeting options, such as interests or demographics, to see which ones generate the most leads.
- Landing pages: Test different landing pages to see which ones have the highest conversion rates.

Once you have identified the elements of your campaigns that are performing best, you can optimize your strategy to maximize your ROI. This may involve increasing your ad spend on high-performing campaigns, refining your targeting, or testing new ad formats.

Optimizing your Quora lead generation campaigns is a critical aspect of maximizing your return on investment (ROI). Once you have identified the elements of your campaigns that are performing best, you can make data-driven decisions to refine your strategy and improve your results.

Increasing ad spend on high-performing campaigns

One way to optimize your Quora lead generation campaigns is to increase your ad spend on campaigns that are generating the most leads. By allocating more budget to your top-performing campaigns, you can increase the number of leads generated and maximize your ROI.

However, it is important to be strategic in how you allocate your ad spend. You should focus on campaigns that have a high conversion rate and a low cost per lead. You should also monitor your metrics regularly to ensure that your ad spend is generating a positive ROI.

Refining targeting

Another way to optimize your Quora lead generation campaigns is to refine your targeting. By targeting the right audience, you can increase the likelihood of generating high-quality leads and reduce your cost per lead.

There are several targeting options available on Quora, including interests, demographics, and behavior. You should test different targeting options to see which ones generate the most leads and refine your targeting based on your results.

For example, if you are targeting users interested in digital marketing, you may want to narrow your targeting to users interested in specific aspects of digital marketing, such as SEO or social media marketing. This can help you reach a more targeted audience and increase the likelihood of generating high-quality leads.

Testing new ad formats

Quora offers several ad formats, including text ads, image ads, and video ads. Testing different ad formats can help you identify the most effective format for generating leads and optimizing your campaigns.

For example, you may find that image ads generate a higher click-through rate (CTR) than text ads or that video ads generate a higher conversion rate than image ads. By testing different ad formats, you can identify the format that resonates best with your target audience and optimize your campaigns accordingly.

You should also test different ad creatives within each ad format to see which ones generate the best results. For example, you may want to test different headlines, descriptions, and images to see which combination generates the highest CTR or conversion rate.

In conclusion, optimizing your Quora lead generation campaigns is critical to maximizing your ROI. By increasing your ad spend on high-performing campaigns, refining your targeting, and testing new ad formats, you can make data-driven decisions to improve your results and generate more high-quality leads. Remember to monitor your metrics regularly and analyze your results to gain insights into your campaigns' effectiveness and make informed decisions to optimize your strategy.

17

Common mistakes to avoid when using Quora for lead generation

Quora is a popular social media platform where people can ask and answer questions. As a digital marketer, you can leverage Quora for lead generation by sharing your expertise, providing value to your audience, and establishing your brand as a thought leader in your industry. However, there are common mistakes that you need to avoid when using Quora for lead generation. In this article, I will discuss some of these mistakes and how to avoid them.

- Failing to identify your target audience

One of the most common mistakes that marketers make when using Quora for lead generation is failing to identify their target audience. It is essential to know who your target audience is so that you can tailor your content to their needs and interests. You should research your audience's demographics, interests, and pain points to create content that resonates with them.

• Not providing value in your answers

Another mistake that marketers make is not providing value in their answers. Quora is not a platform for self-promotion. It is a platform where people come to seek answers to their questions. Your answers should be informative, helpful, and insightful. Your primary goal should be to provide value to your audience, not to promote your brand.

• Over-promoting your brand

While it is essential to promote your brand on Quora, you should avoid over-promoting it. Over-promoting your brand can make you appear spammy and pushy. Instead, focus on providing value to your audience and building relationships with them. As you establish yourself as a thought leader in your industry, your audience will naturally be drawn to your brand.

• Failing to optimize your profile

Your Quora profile is an essential part of your lead generation strategy. Your profile should be optimized to attract your target audience. Your profile should include a professional photo, a concise bio that highlights your expertise, and links to your website and social media profiles. You should also include your industry keywords in your profile to make it easier for people to find you.

• Not monitoring your analytics

To determine the effectiveness of your lead generation strategy on Quora, you should monitor your analytics regularly. Quora provides analytics that show you how many views and upvotes your answers receive, how many followers you have, and how many clicks your links get. By monitoring your analytics, you can identify what content resonates with your audience and adjust your strategy accordingly.

- Not engaging with your audience

Engaging with your audience is critical to building relationships and establishing trust. When someone upvotes your answer or leaves a comment, respond to them promptly. Engage in conversations with your audience, answer their questions, and offer additional insights. By engaging with your audience, you can establish yourself as a thought leader and build a loyal following.

- Not promoting your Quora content

Promoting your Quora content on your website and social media platforms can help you reach a broader audience and generate more leads. Share your Quora answers on your social media profiles and link to them on your website. This can help you drive traffic to your Quora profile and increase your visibility on the platform.

- Failing to follow Quora's guidelines

Quora has strict guidelines that you must follow to avoid being flagged or banned from the platform. For example, you should not post spammy or low-quality content, use inappropriate language, or engage in fraudulent activities. Make sure you read and follow Quora's guidelines to ensure that your account remains in good standing.

In conclusion, Quora can be an effective platform for lead generation if used correctly. To avoid common mistakes, identify your target audience, provide value in your answers, avoid over-promoting your brand, optimize your profile, monitor your analytics, engage with your audience, promote your Quora content, and follow Quora's guidelines

18

How to stay up-to-date with Quora's algorithm changes

s a digital marketer, staying up-to-date with algorithm changes on platforms like Quora is critical to maintaining a successful marketing strategy. Quora is a popular question-and-answer platform with over 300 million monthly active users. It is a great platform to connect with your audience and establish thought leadership, but it is constantly changing its algorithm to improve user experience and engagement.

Here are some tips on how to stay up-to-date with Quora's algorithm changes:

1. Follow Quora's official blog and social media channels Quora regularly publishes blog posts and updates on its official blog and social media channels. Following these channels can help you stay informed about any algorithm changes, new features, or updates on the platform. You can also sign up for Quora's newsletter to get updates directly in your inbox.

2. Keep an eye on your analytics Monitoring your Quora analytics can give you valuable insights into how your content is performing on the platform. You can see which answers are getting the most views, upvotes, and shares. By analyzing your analytics, you can identify any changes in your performance and adjust your strategy accordingly.

3. Join Quora's partner program Quora's partner program is designed to help creators monetize their content on the platform. As a partner, you will get access to advanced analytics, exclusive features, and early access to new tools and updates. You will also get regular updates from Quora about algorithm changes and best practices for content creation.

4. Engage with the Quora community Engaging with the Quora community can help you stay up-to-date with the latest trends and topics on the platform. Following popular topics, answering questions, and participating in discussions can give you a better understanding of the type of content that performs well on Quora. You can also connect with other Quora users and learn from their experiences and insights.

5. Use Quora's Ad Manager Quora's Ad Manager is a powerful tool that can help you reach your target audience and promote your content on the platform. As a marketer, using Quora's Ad Manager can give you a better understanding of how the algorithm works and how you can optimize your content for maximum visibility and engagement.

6. Stay informed about SEO best practices Quora's algorithm is heavily influenced by SEO best practices. By staying informed about the latest SEO trends and best practices,

you can optimize your content for both search engines and Quora's algorithm. You should also be familiar with Quora's guidelines for content creation, which include avoiding spammy or promotional content and providing valuable and informative answers to users' questions.

In conclusion, staying up-to-date with Quora's algorithm changes is essential for any digital marketer looking to leverage the platform for marketing purposes. By following these tips, you can stay informed about any updates or changes to the algorithm and adjust your strategy accordingly. Remember to always focus on providing valuable and informative content to users and following best practices for content creation and SEO. With the right strategy and approach, Quora can be a powerful tool for driving traffic, engagement, and conversions for your business.

19

The importance of engaging with Quora users to generate leads

I n today's fast-paced digital world, generating leads is crucial for any business looking to grow and expand. With so many platforms available to marketers, it can be challenging to determine which ones will provide the most return on investment. One platform that has gained significant traction over the past few years is Quora, a question-and-answer website with a community of over 300 million monthly active users. Engaging with Quora users can be a valuable strategy for generating leads, and in this article, we will explore why.

Firstly, Quora offers a unique opportunity for businesses to connect with their target audience. Users come to Quora to ask questions and seek advice from experts in various fields, including business and marketing. By answering questions related to your industry, you can establish yourself as an authority in your niche and gain the trust of potential customers. By engaging with users on Quora, you can build relationships that may lead to long-term business partnerships.

Secondly, Quora provides a platform for businesses to show-case their expertise and knowledge. By answering questions related to your industry, you can demonstrate your understanding of the subject matter and provide valuable insights to potential customers. This can help you to establish a reputation as a thought leader in your field and increase your brand's visibility.

Thirdly, Quora can drive traffic to your website. By including links to your website in your answers, you can direct interested users to your site, where they can learn more about your products or services. This can help to increase the number of qualified leads in your sales funnel, ultimately leading to increased revenue for your business.

To effectively engage with Quora users and generate leads, there are several best practices to keep in mind. Firstly, it's important to identify the questions that your target audience is asking on Quora. By researching popular topics and questions related to your industry, you can create a list of questions to answer and develop a content strategy to address these topics.

Secondly, when answering questions on Quora, it's essential to provide value to the user. This means answering the question thoroughly and providing actionable advice or insights. Avoid using your answer as an opportunity to promote your products or services, as this can come across as spammy and may harm your reputation on the platform.

Thirdly, it's crucial to engage with users in a genuine and authentic way. Respond to comments on your answers and engage in conversations with users who express interest in your business or industry. By building relationships with users on Quora, you can establish a network of potential customers and referral sources.

Fourthly, be consistent with your engagement on Quora.

Regularly answering questions and engaging with users can help to keep your brand top-of-mind for potential customers. It's also essential to monitor your Quora activity regularly, as this can provide valuable insights into user behavior and preferences.

Lastly, track your results to determine the effectiveness of your Quora engagement strategy. Use analytics tools to track the number of views, upvotes, and clicks on your answers, as well as the number of leads generated from Quora. This can help you to refine your strategy and optimize your results over time.

In conclusion, engaging with Quora users can be an effective strategy for generating leads and building relationships with potential customers. By providing value and demonstrating your expertise, you can establish yourself as a thought leader in your field and increase your brand's visibility. With the right approach and consistent effort, Quora can be a valuable tool in your lead generation arsenal.

20

How to identify and target high-value leads on Quora

As a digital marketer, one of the most important tasks is identifying and targeting high-value leads on various platforms. Quora, with its large user base and active community, can be a valuable source of high-quality leads. However, to effectively identify and target these leads, you need to have a clear strategy in place.

Here are some tips on how to identify and target high-value leads on Quora:

1. Identify your target audience The first step in identifying and targeting high-value leads on Quora is to clearly define your target audience. Who are you trying to reach? What are their interests, needs, and pain points? Once you have a clear understanding of your target audience, you can start looking for questions and topics that are relevant to them.

2. Use Quora search Quora search is a powerful tool that can help you find relevant questions and topics related to your

target audience. You can search for keywords related to your product or service, and Quora will return a list of questions and topics that are related to those keywords. You can then filter the results based on various criteria, such as the number of followers or the number of upvotes.

3. Look for high-value questions Once you have identified your target audience and used Quora search to find relevant questions and topics, you need to focus on high-value questions. High-value questions are those that have a large number of followers and are highly relevant to your target audience. These questions are a great opportunity to showcase your expertise and engage with potential leads.

4. Provide value in your answers When answering questions on Quora, it's important to provide value to the person asking the question. This means providing a detailed and thoughtful answer that addresses the question directly. You should also provide links to additional resources or information that can help the person asking the question. By providing value in your answers, you can build trust and credibility with potential leads.

5. Engage with potential leads Engaging with potential leads on Quora is an important part of the process. This means responding to comments and questions, and offering to connect with people outside of Quora. You can also use Quora's messaging system to reach out to potential leads directly. By engaging with potential leads, you can build relationships and establish yourself as a trusted authority in your field.

6. Monitor your performance Finally, it's important to monitor your performance on Quora to ensure that you are targeting high-value leads effectively. You can use Quora's

analytics tools to track the performance of your answers, including the number of views and upvotes. You can also track the performance of your profile, including the number of followers and the engagement rate. By monitoring your performance, you can identify areas for improvement and optimize your strategy accordingly.

In conclusion, identifying and targeting high-value leads on Quora requires a clear strategy and a deep understanding of your target audience. By using Quora search, focusing on high-value questions, providing value in your answers, engaging with potential leads, and monitoring your performance, you can effectively identify and target high-value leads on this platform. As with any marketing strategy, it's important to be patient and persistent, and to continuously refine your approach based on the results you see.

21

Tips for creating compelling Quora content that generates leads

As a digital marketer, I've found Quora to be a valuable platform for generating leads and increasing brand awareness. Quora is a question-and-answer website where users can ask and answer questions on various topics. With over 300 million active users, Quora presents a unique opportunity for businesses to engage with their target audience and establish themselves as industry experts. In this article, I'll share some tips for creating compelling Quora content that generates leads.

- Identify your target audience

The first step to creating compelling Quora content is to identify your target audience. This will help you understand the type of content that will resonate with them and the questions they are asking. Use Quora's search function to find questions related to your industry or niche. Look for questions with a significant number of views and upvotes, as this indicates that the question is popular and relevant to your target audience.

- Provide value

When answering questions on Quora, it's important to provide value to the reader. Your answer should be informative, helpful, and provide insights that the reader may not have known before. This will position you as an industry expert and increase the likelihood that the reader will click on your profile to learn more about your business.

- Keep it concise

While it's important to provide value in your answer, it's equally important to keep it concise. Quora users are typically looking for quick answers to their questions, so avoid long-winded responses that may lose the reader's attention. Keep your answer to the point, and use bullet points or numbered lists to break up the text and make it more readable.

- Use visuals

Visuals such as images, screenshots, and videos can help to make your answer more engaging and informative. For example, if you're answering a question about how to use a particular software tool, including a screenshot or video tutorial can help to illustrate your answer and make it more actionable for the reader.

- Include relevant links

Including relevant links in your answer can help to provide additional value to the reader and drive traffic to your website. For example, if you're answering a question about the benefits of using a particular product, you could include a link to your website where the reader can learn more and potentially make a purchase.

- Be authentic

One of the key benefits of Quora is that it allows businesses to establish themselves as industry experts and thought leaders. However, this can only be achieved if you are authentic and transparent in your answers. Avoid overly promotional language and focus on providing value to the reader. If you come across as genuine and helpful, readers are more likely to trust and engage with your content.

- Engage with the community

Engaging with the Quora community can help to increase your visibility and credibility on the platform. Respond to comments on your answers, follow other users in your industry or niche, and participate in relevant discussions. This will help to establish you as an active member of the community and increase the likelihood that users will click on your profile to learn more about your business.

- Analyze your performance

Finally, it's important to analyze your performance on Quora to understand what's working and what's not. Use Quora's analytics tools to track the performance of your answers, including the number of views, upvotes, and shares. This will help you to identify which types of content are resonating with your target audience and adjust your strategy accordingly.

In conclusion, Quora presents a unique opportunity for businesses to engage with their target audience and establish themselves as industry experts. By following these tips for creating compelling Quora content, you can generate leads and increase brand awareness on the platform.

22

The role of Quora in building brand awareness and trust

As a digital marketer, I have seen firsthand the power of Quora in building brand awareness and trust. Quora is a popular question-and-answer platform that provides users with an opportunity to ask and answer questions on a variety of topics. With over 300 million monthly active users, Quora is an excellent platform for businesses looking to expand their reach and connect with potential customers.

One of the most significant advantages of Quora is its ability to generate brand awareness. By answering questions related to your industry or niche, you can establish yourself as an expert in the field and build credibility with potential customers. When users see your answers, they become more aware of your brand and what it has to offer.

Another way Quora helps build brand awareness is through the use of keywords. By using relevant keywords in your answers, you can help your brand appear in search results when users search for those terms. This can increase your brand's visibility and attract more potential customers to your business.

In addition to generating brand awareness, Quora can also help businesses build trust with their audience. By providing valuable and informative answers to users' questions, businesses can establish themselves as authorities in their respective industries. When users see that a business is knowledgeable and helpful, they are more likely to trust that business and consider it when making purchasing decisions.

Another way Quora helps build trust is by allowing businesses to engage with their audience in a more personal way. By answering users' questions and providing helpful information, businesses can build relationships with their audience and establish themselves as approachable and friendly. This can go a long way in building trust and loyalty with potential customers.

To make the most of Quora as a digital marketer, it's important to keep a few best practices in mind. First, it's essential to ensure that your answers are high-quality and informative. The more value you can provide to users, the more likely they are to trust your brand and consider it when making purchasing decisions.

Second, it's important to be consistent in your use of Quora. Regularly answering questions and engaging with users can help you build a strong presence on the platform and establish yourself as an authority in your industry.

Third, it's essential to use keywords effectively. By using relevant keywords in your answers, you can help your brand appear in search results and attract more potential customers to your business.

Fourth, it's important to engage with other users on the platform. By commenting on other users' answers and asking questions, you can build relationships and establish yourself as a valuable member of the Quora community.

Finally, it's important to be authentic and transparent in your use of Quora. Users can easily spot businesses that are trying to promote themselves or push their products, so it's essential to be genuine and helpful in your interactions with users.

In conclusion, Quora is an excellent platform for businesses looking to build brand awareness and trust. By providing valuable answers to users' questions and engaging with the Quora community, businesses can establish themselves as authorities in their respective industries and build credibility with potential customers. To make the most of Quora as a digital marketer, it's important to be consistent, use keywords effectively, engage with other users, and be authentic and transparent in your interactions with users.

23

Strategies for leveraging Quora to drive website traffic and leads

As a digital marketer, one of the most important tasks is to drive traffic and leads to your website. In today's digital age, there are a variety of channels to explore, from social media to paid search, but one platform that often goes overlooked is Quora. Quora is a question-and-answer site that allows users to ask and answer questions on a variety of topics. With over 300 million monthly active users, Quora is an untapped goldmine for marketers to drive website traffic and leads. In this article, we will discuss strategies for leveraging Quora to drive website traffic and leads.

- Identify Relevant Topics and Questions

The first step in leveraging Quora to drive website traffic and leads is to identify relevant topics and questions. You can use Quora's search function to find topics related to your business, industry, or niche. Once you've found a topic, you can explore the questions related to that topic. Look for questions that have a high number of views and followers. These are the questions that are likely to attract a lot of attention and generate traffic to your website.

• Create High-Quality Answers

Once you've identified relevant topics and questions, the next step is to create high-quality answers. Your answers should be informative, engaging, and helpful to the Quora community. Avoid using overly promotional language and focus on providing value to the reader. Your goal is to establish yourself as an authority in your industry and build trust with potential customers.

• Include Relevant Links in Your Answers

One of the key strategies for driving website traffic and leads from Quora is to include relevant links in your answers. These links could be to your website, blog, landing pages, or other relevant resources. However, it's important to avoid spamming or overly promoting your links. Make sure the links are relevant to the question and answer and provide value to the reader.

• Leverage Quora Ads

Another way to drive website traffic and leads from Quora is to leverage Quora Ads. Quora Ads allows you to target specific audiences based on topics, questions, and demographics. You can also create different ad formats, such as text ads, image ads, and sponsored content. Quora Ads can be a highly effective way to drive targeted traffic to your website and generate leads.

- Monitor Your Results and Adjust Your Strategy

As with any marketing strategy, it's important to monitor your results and adjust your strategy accordingly. Use Quora's analytics tools to track the performance of your answers and ads. Look for patterns in your traffic and leads and adjust your strategy based on what's working and what's not. This will help you to continually improve your Quora marketing efforts and maximize your results.

- Engage with the Quora Community

Finally, one of the most important strategies for leveraging Quora to drive website traffic and leads is to engage with the Quora community. This means not only answering questions but also commenting on other answers and questions. By engaging with the Quora community, you can establish yourself as an authority and build relationships with potential customers. This can help to drive traffic to your website and generate leads over the long term.

In conclusion, Quora is a highly underrated platform for driving website traffic and leads. By identifying relevant topics and questions, creating high-quality answers, including relevant links, leveraging Quora Ads, monitoring your results, and engaging with the Quora community, you can drive targeted traffic to your website and generate leads. With over 300 million monthly active users, Quora is a platform that digital marketers cannot afford to overlook.

24

How to use Quora to generate leads for different industries

Q uora is a popular question and answer platform that allows users to ask, answer, and follow questions on various topics. With over 300 million active users, it provides an excellent opportunity for businesses to generate leads and engage with potential customers. In this article, I will explain how to use Quora to generate leads for different industries.

1. Identify relevant topics and questions The first step to using Quora for lead generation is to identify relevant topics and questions related to your industry. Search for questions related to your product or service and follow those topics. You can also create your own topics related to your industry or product. This will allow you to monitor the questions and engage with potential customers.

2. Answer questions and provide value Once you have identified relevant topics and questions, start answering them. Provide valuable and informative answers that address

the question asked. Make sure that your answers are clear, concise, and easy to understand. Use examples and provide links to your website or blog for further information. This will establish your expertise in the industry and help build trust with potential customers.

3. Use targeted keywords Using targeted keywords in your answers can help increase visibility and generate more leads. Use relevant keywords in your answers and make sure they are incorporated naturally. Do not overuse keywords as this may make your answers sound spammy and turn off potential customers.

4. Use call-to-action (CTA) in your answers Adding a call-to-action (CTA) in your answers can help generate leads. Ask the reader to take action such as visiting your website or signing up for a newsletter. Make sure that your CTA is relevant to the question asked and provides value to the reader.

5. Engage with potential customers Engage with potential customers by responding to their comments and questions. This will help build a relationship with them and establish trust. Respond to comments promptly and provide additional information if needed. This will help build credibility and increase the chances of generating a lead.

6. Monitor results and adjust your strategy Monitor the results of your Quora activity and adjust your strategy accordingly. Track the number of views, upvotes, and clicks on your links. Analyze which topics and questions are generating the most leads and adjust your strategy accordingly. This will help you optimize your Quora activity and generate more leads over time.

7. Use Quora Ads Quora Ads is an advertising platform that

allows businesses to target potential customers based on their interests and behaviors. It provides an excellent opportunity for businesses to generate leads and increase brand awareness. Use Quora Ads to target specific audiences and promote your product or service. Make sure that your ads are relevant and provide value to the reader.

8. Use Quora Spaces Quora Spaces is a new feature that allows businesses to create their own private discussion groups related to their industry or product. This provides an excellent opportunity for businesses to engage with potential customers and generate leads. Use Quora Spaces to create a community around your product or service and provide value to members. Make sure that your content is informative and engaging.

9. Build your profile and credibility Building your profile and credibility on Quora is essential for generating leads. Make sure that your profile is complete and provides information about your expertise and experience. Use your real name and a professional profile picture. This will help build trust with potential customers and establish your credibility in the industry.

In conclusion, Quora provides an excellent opportunity for businesses to generate leads and engage with potential customers. Identify relevant topics and questions, answer them with valuable content, use targeted keywords, add a call-to-action, engage with potential customers, monitor results, use Quora Ads, use Quora Spaces, and build your profile and credibility.

25

The benefits of collaborating with other Quora users for lead generation

As a digital marketer, I have found that collaborating with other Quora users can be an effective way to generate leads and drive business growth. Quora is a question-and-answer platform where users can ask and answer questions on a wide range of topics. By collaborating with other Quora users, you can tap into their expertise and audience to expand your reach and attract new leads.

Here are some of the key benefits of collaborating with other Quora users for lead generation:

- Increased visibility and credibility

Collaborating with other Quora users can help you increase your visibility on the platform. When you partner with other users, you can leverage their audience to reach new people who may be interested in your products or services. This can help you build your brand and establish yourself as a credible expert in your industry.

- Access to new leads and customers

Partnering with other Quora users can also help you access new leads and customers. By working with other users, you can tap into their existing audience and reach people who may not have heard of your business before. This can help you expand your reach and attract new customers who are interested in what you have to offer.

- Collaboration leads to more high-quality content

When you collaborate with other Quora users, you have the opportunity to create high-quality content that is informative and engaging. By pooling your expertise and knowledge, you can produce content that is more valuable to your target audience. This can help you attract more leads and establish yourself as a trusted authority in your industry.

- Builds strong relationships with fellow experts in your field

Collaborating with other Quora users can also help you build strong relationships with other experts in your field. This can lead to new opportunities for partnerships, joint ventures, and other collaborations in the future. Building strong relationships with other experts can also help you stay up-to-date on industry trends and best practices.

- Drives traffic to your website or landing pages

Finally, collaborating with other Quora users can help you drive traffic to your website or landing pages. By creating valuable content together, you can encourage users to click through to your website or landing pages to learn more about your products or services. This can help you generate more leads and increase your conversion rates.

Overall, collaborating with other Quora users can be a powerful way to generate leads and drive business growth. By working together, you can tap into each other's expertise and audience to expand your reach and attract new customers. So, if you're looking to boost your lead generation efforts, consider collaborating with other Quora users and see how it can benefit your business.

26

How to use Quora's analytics to track your lead generation progress

Q uora is a popular social networking platform where users can ask and answer questions on a variety of topics. As a digital marketer, you can use Quora to generate leads and drive traffic to your website. However, to get the best results, you need to track your lead generation progress. In this article, we will explore how to use Quora's analytics to do just that.

1. Set Up Conversion Tracking The first step is to set up conversion tracking on your website. This will allow you to track the number of leads and sales that come from Quora. To set up conversion tracking, you will need to add a tracking code to your website. You can use Google Analytics or any other tracking software of your choice. Once you have set up conversion tracking, you can track the number of leads and sales that come from Quora.

2. Use Quora's Analytics Dashboard Quora has an analytics dashboard that allows you to track your lead generation

progress. To access the dashboard, go to your profile and click on the "Analytics" tab. Here, you will see various metrics such as views, upvotes, and clicks.

3. Track Your Views and Upvotes The number of views and upvotes your answers receive is an indication of their popularity. The more views and upvotes your answers get, the more exposure you will get, and the more likely you are to generate leads. Use the analytics dashboard to track your views and upvotes and see which answers are performing well.

4. Monitor Your Clicks Clicks are another crucial metric to track. They indicate how many people are clicking on the links in your answers and visiting your website. Use the analytics dashboard to track your clicks and see which answers are generating the most clicks.

5. Monitor Your Conversions The ultimate goal of lead generation is to convert visitors into leads and customers. Use the conversion tracking you set up earlier to track your conversions. This will allow you to see how many leads and sales are coming from Quora.

6. Analyze Your Data Once you have gathered enough data, it's time to analyze it. Look at which answers are generating the most views, upvotes, clicks, and conversions. Identify any trends or patterns that emerge. Use this information to refine your Quora strategy and create more effective answers.

In conclusion, Quora's analytics dashboard is a powerful tool for tracking your lead generation progress. Use it to monitor your views, upvotes, clicks, and conversions. Analyze the data to identify trends and refine your strategy. By doing so, you will be able to generate more leads and drive more traffic to your website.

27

The role of Quora in B2B lead generation

As an experienced digital marketer, I can attest that Quora plays a significant role in B2B lead generation. Quora is a social media platform that allows users to ask and answer questions on a range of topics, making it a valuable resource for businesses to engage with their target audience and establish themselves as thought leaders in their respective industries.

One of the primary benefits of using Quora for B2B lead generation is the opportunity to connect with potential customers who are actively seeking information on products or services related to your business. By monitoring relevant topics and questions on Quora, businesses can identify opportunities to provide valuable insights and position themselves as experts in their field. This, in turn, can help to build trust with potential customers and increase the likelihood of them considering your business as a solution provider.

Additionally, Quora can be an effective tool for driving traffic to a company's website. By including links to relevant content on their website in their answers on Quora, businesses can direct interested parties to their website and potentially convert them into leads or customers. This can be especially effective when answering questions that are highly relevant to the products or services offered by the business.

Another benefit of using Quora for B2B lead generation is the ability to conduct market research and gain insights into the needs and preferences of your target audience. By analyzing the questions and discussions on Quora related to your industry, businesses can gain a better understanding of the pain points and challenges faced by potential customers, and tailor their marketing efforts accordingly.

It's important to note that the key to success with Quora as a lead generation tool lies in providing high-quality, valuable answers that genuinely help the person asking the question. Simply promoting your business or products without providing any real value is unlikely to result in meaningful lead generation. By consistently providing helpful, insightful answers and establishing yourself as a trusted authority in your industry, you can build a loyal following on Quora and generate a steady stream of leads for your business.

In conclusion, Quora can be a valuable tool for B2B lead generation, providing opportunities to connect with potential customers, drive traffic to your website, and gain valuable insights into your target audience. By approaching Quora with a strategic mindset and a focus on providing value to your audience, businesses can establish themselves as thought leaders in their industry and generate meaningful leads for their business.

28

The role of Quora in B2C lead generation

Quora, the question-and-answer platform, has emerged as a popular destination for users seeking information on various topics. As a digital marketer, leveraging Quora as a lead generation channel can be an effective strategy for B2C businesses. In this article, we will explore the role of Quora in B2C lead generation and the tactics that can be employed to maximize its potential.

Why Quora for B2C Lead Generation?

Quora is an ideal platform for B2C lead generation due to its vast user base and its reputation as a credible source of information. With over 300 million monthly active users, Quora presents an opportunity for businesses to reach a large audience and establish their authority in their industry. Additionally, users on Quora are actively seeking information and are often open to exploring solutions to their problems. This makes Quora an ideal platform to showcase products and services that can help solve their pain points.

Tactics for B2C Lead Generation on Quora

1. Establishing Authority:

One of the key tactics for B2C lead generation on Quora is to establish authority in your industry. By answering questions related to your industry and providing valuable insights, you can position yourself as a thought leader and earn the trust of potential customers. Additionally, you can add a bio to your Quora profile that showcases your expertise and includes a link to your website, making it easy for users to learn more about your business.

1. Targeting Relevant Questions:

To maximize the potential of Quora for B2C lead generation, it is important to target relevant questions. By identifying questions that are relevant to your business and your target audience, you can provide valuable answers that position your products or services as a solution to their problems. You can use keyword research to identify relevant questions and topics, and monitor the Quora feed to stay up to date on the latest trends and discussions in your industry.

1. Providing Value:

When answering questions on Quora, it is important to focus on providing value to the user rather than promoting your products or services directly. By providing insightful and helpful answers, you can establish trust with potential customers and position your business as a credible source of information. Additionally, you can include a call-to-action at the end of your answer, directing users to your website or offering additional resources to learn more.

1. Engaging with Users:

Engaging with users on Quora can also be an effective tactic for B2C lead generation. By following users who are relevant to your business and engaging with their content, you can establish relationships and build a community around your brand. Additionally, you can participate in discussions related to your industry and answer follow-up questions to further establish your authority and credibility.

Measuring Success on Quora

To measure the success of your B2C lead generation efforts on Quora, it is important to track metrics such as views, upvotes, and clicks on your website link. Additionally, you can monitor the quality of the leads generated from Quora by tracking metrics such as lead quality, conversion rates, and customer lifetime value.

Conclusion

Quora presents a valuable opportunity for B2C businesses to generate leads and establish their authority in their industry. By leveraging tactics such as establishing authority, targeting relevant questions, providing value, and engaging with users, businesses can maximize the potential of Quora for lead generation. By measuring success through relevant metrics, businesses can continue to refine their approach and optimize their results over time.

29

Using Quora to generate leads for B2C businesses

Q uora is a popular question-and-answer website that attracts millions of users every day. As a digital marketer, you can use Quora to generate leads for B2C businesses. In this article, we will explore how you can use Quora to generate leads and increase sales.

1. Create a Quora Account and Build Your Reputation The first step to using Quora to generate leads is to create an account and build your reputation. You can do this by answering questions related to your business niche, and providing valuable insights and advice to other users. By doing this, you establish yourself as an expert in your field, and people are more likely to trust your advice and follow your recommendations.

2. Identify Your Target Audience To generate leads on Quora, you need to identify your target audience. Look for questions related to your business niche and answer them with valuable insights and advice. By doing this, you

attract people who are interested in your products or services, and they are more likely to become leads.

3. Use Your Answers to Generate Traffic To generate leads on Quora, you need to use your answers to drive traffic to your website or landing pages. Include links to your website or landing pages in your answers, and encourage users to click on them for more information. By doing this, you increase your website traffic and generate more leads.

4. Engage with Other Users Engage with other users on Quora to increase your visibility and attract more leads. Follow other users in your niche and upvote their answers. Comment on their answers and provide additional insights and advice. By doing this, you establish yourself as an expert in your field and build relationships with other users.

5. Use Quora Ads Quora Ads is an effective way to generate leads for B2C businesses. You can use Quora Ads to target specific audiences based on their interests, location, and other demographics. Quora Ads can also be used to promote your answers and increase visibility for your brand.

6. Measure Your Results To optimize your Quora lead generation strategy, you need to measure your results. Use analytics tools to track your website traffic, click-through rates, and conversion rates. This information will help you identify what works and what doesn't work, and make adjustments to your strategy accordingly.

In conclusion, Quora is a powerful tool for generating leads for B2C businesses. By building your reputation, identifying your target audience, using your answers to generate traffic, engaging with other users, using Quora Ads, and measuring your results, you can increase your website traffic, generate more leads, and increase your sales.

30

The importance of personalization in Quora lead generation

As a digital marketer, I can attest to the fact that personalization plays a critical role in the success of any lead generation campaign on Quora. With over 300 million monthly active users, Quora has become a goldmine for businesses looking to generate leads and drive sales. However, to make the most of the platform, it's essential to personalize your approach to each user and tailor your messaging accordingly.

Here are a few reasons why personalization is so important in Quora lead generation:

1. Builds Trust and Credibility Personalization helps build trust and credibility with potential leads. By addressing them by their name or referencing their previous interactions with your brand, you're showing that you value their input and are genuinely interested in their needs. When users feel seen and heard, they're more likely to engage with your content and consider your offering.

2. Increases Engagement Quora is a platform that thrives on engagement. Personalization can help increase the engagement of your content by making it more relevant to each user. For example, if you're promoting a product or service, tailoring your message to their specific needs or interests can help grab their attention and entice them to learn more.

3. Improves Conversion Rates Personalization can improve conversion rates by making your messaging more persuasive and compelling. When users feel that your offer is relevant to their needs, they're more likely to take action and become a lead. By customizing your messaging, you can also help overcome any objections or barriers that may be preventing users from converting.

4. Reduces Wasted Ad Spend Personalization can also help reduce wasted ad spend by targeting your messaging to users who are more likely to convert. By understanding each user's behavior and preferences, you can tailor your content to reach the most qualified leads, which can help reduce the cost per lead and improve ROI.

So, how can you personalize your approach to lead generation on Quora? Here are a few tips:

1. Use Quora's Ad Targeting Options Quora offers several ad targeting options that can help you reach the most qualified leads. You can target users based on their interests, location, device, and more. By using these options, you can ensure that your content is reaching the right users at the right time.

2. Address Users by Their Name Personalization can start

with something as simple as addressing users by their name. Quora allows you to customize your ad copy to include the user's name, which can help grab their attention and make your messaging more personal.

3. Reference Users' Interests and Behaviors Quora also allows you to target users based on their interests and behaviors. By referencing these in your messaging, you can make your content more relevant and increase engagement.

4. Use Dynamic Creative Quora's dynamic creative feature allows you to customize your ad creative based on the user's behavior or preferences. For example, you can display different images or messaging depending on the user's location or device.

In conclusion, personalization is critical in Quora lead generation. By tailoring your messaging to each user, you can build trust, increase engagement, improve conversion rates, and reduce wasted ad spend. To make the most of the platform, be sure to take advantage of Quora's ad targeting options and personalize your messaging accordingly.

31

How to nurture leads generated on Quora

A s a digital marketer with extensive experience, I can confidently say that Quora is a powerful platform for generating high-quality leads. However, it's important to note that lead generation is only half the battle. Nurturing those leads is just as important, if not more so. In this article, I'll share my top tips on how to nurture leads generated on Quora.

1. Follow up quickly: The first step in nurturing leads is to follow up with them as soon as possible. When someone asks a question related to your product or service on Quora, and you provide a helpful answer, it's likely that they will be interested in learning more. Don't wait too long to reach out to them - strike while the iron is hot!

2. Provide more value: Once you've made initial contact with your lead, the next step is to provide even more value. Remember, they came to Quora seeking information and advice, so give them just that. Share additional insights, resources, and tips that will help them better understand

your offering and how it can benefit them.

3. Build a relationship: As you continue to provide value, focus on building a relationship with your lead. Ask them questions, listen to their concerns, and tailor your communication to their needs and interests. The goal here is to create a sense of trust and rapport, which will make them more likely to convert into a paying customer down the line.

4. Educate, don't sell: One common mistake that many marketers make when nurturing leads is to focus too much on selling. Remember, your lead is still in the research phase and may not be ready to make a purchase just yet. Instead of pushing your product or service too aggressively, focus on educating them and helping them make an informed decision.

5. Use retargeting: Another effective way to nurture leads generated on Quora is to use retargeting. By placing a tracking pixel on your website, you can show ads to people who have already interacted with your brand. This can help keep your brand top of mind and encourage them to take action.

6. Personalize your content: Finally, make sure that you're personalizing your content to your lead's needs and interests. Use data and insights to understand what topics they're most interested in and tailor your content accordingly. This can include everything from blog posts and whitepapers to webinars and case studies.

In conclusion, nurturing leads generated on Quora requires a strategic approach that focuses on building relationships, providing value, and educating your audience. By following the tips outlined above, you can maximize your chances of converting these leads into loyal customers over time.

32

The role of Quora in building customer relationships

Q uora is a popular question-and-answer platform that allows people to ask and answer questions on a wide range of topics. As a digital marketer, I have found that Quora can be an effective tool for building customer relationships.

One of the key advantages of Quora is its ability to help brands establish themselves as thought leaders in their respective industries. By providing valuable insights and answering relevant questions, businesses can demonstrate their expertise and build credibility with potential customers.

To make the most of Quora, it is important to start by identifying the key topics and questions that are relevant to your brand. This involves conducting research to understand the most commonly asked questions in your industry and identifying areas where you can provide unique insights.

Once you have identified the key topics and questions, it is important to focus on providing high-quality, informative answers that add value to the conversation. This involves taking the time to craft thoughtful responses that address the question at hand and provide actionable insights for the reader.

In addition to establishing thought leadership, Quora can also be an effective tool for building direct relationships with potential customers. By engaging with users who ask questions related to your business, you can start a conversation and establish a connection with them.

This can be particularly effective if you are able to provide personalized advice or recommendations based on the user's specific situation. By demonstrating that you are invested in their success and willing to go above and beyond to help them, you can build a strong foundation for a long-term customer relationship.

Another benefit of Quora is its ability to drive traffic to your website. By including links to relevant blog posts or landing pages in your answers, you can encourage users to visit your website and learn more about your products or services.

To make the most of this opportunity, it is important to ensure that the content you are linking to is high-quality and relevant to the user's question. This can help to build trust and establish your brand as a valuable resource in your industry.

Overall, the role of Quora in building customer relationships is significant. By providing valuable insights, engaging with potential customers, and driving traffic to your website, Quora can be an effective tool for building trust and establishing long-term relationships with your target audience.

33

Case studies of successful Quora lead generation campaigns

Q uora is a popular question-and-answer platform that offers an excellent opportunity for digital marketers to generate leads. With over 300 million active users, Quora is a goldmine for businesses that are looking to attract potential customers and increase brand visibility. In this article, we'll take a closer look at some of the successful Quora lead generation campaigns that have helped businesses achieve their marketing objectives.

1. HubSpot:

HubSpot is a popular inbound marketing platform that offers a range of tools to help businesses attract, engage, and delight their customers. To generate leads on Quora, HubSpot focused on providing valuable answers to questions related to marketing, sales, and customer service. By positioning themselves as thought leaders in the industry, HubSpot was able to attract potential customers to their website and convert them into leads.

One of the keys to HubSpot's success on Quora was their focus on providing high-quality, informative content that was tailored to the needs of their target audience. They also made it a point to engage with their followers by responding to comments and asking follow-up questions, which helped to build trust and establish relationships with their audience.

1. Neil Patel:

Neil Patel is a well-known digital marketing expert who has built a successful business around his personal brand. To generate leads on Quora, Patel focused on answering questions related to SEO, content marketing, and social media marketing. His answers were often lengthy and detailed, providing readers with valuable insights and actionable advice.

In addition to providing high-quality content, Patel also made it a point to include links to his website and other resources that would be useful to his audience. This helped to drive traffic to his website and increase his visibility on Quora.

1. Ahrefs:

Ahrefs is a popular SEO tool that helps businesses improve their search engine rankings and drive more traffic to their website. To generate leads on Quora, Ahrefs focused on answering questions related to SEO, link building, and keyword research. Their answers were often accompanied by data and statistics, which helped to establish their credibility and expertise in the industry.

Ahrefs also made it a point to engage with their audience

by responding to comments and asking follow-up questions. This helped to build relationships with their followers and establish Ahrefs as a trusted source of information in the SEO community.

1. Buffer:

Buffer is a social media management platform that helps businesses schedule and publish content across multiple social media platforms. To generate leads on Quora, Buffer focused on answering questions related to social media marketing, content creation, and audience engagement. Their answers were often accompanied by examples and case studies, which helped to illustrate their points and provide readers with practical advice.

Buffer also made it a point to engage with their audience by responding to comments and asking follow-up questions. This helped to build trust and establish relationships with their followers, which in turn helped to drive more traffic to their website.

In conclusion, Quora is an excellent platform for generating leads and building brand visibility. The key to success on Quora is to provide high-quality, informative content that is tailored to the needs of your target audience. By engaging with your followers and building relationships with them, you can establish yourself as a thought leader in your industry and attract potential customers to your website.